Green and Pleasant Land

POETRY OF THE ENGLISH COUNTRYSIDE

PICTURES BY GORDON BENINGFIELD

Viking

VIKING

Published by the Penguin Group
27 Wrights Lane, London W8 5TZ, England
Viking Penguin Inc., 40 West 23rd Street, New York, New York 10010, USA
Penguin Books Australia Ltd, Ringwood, Victoria, Australia
Penguin Books Canada Ltd, 2801 John Street, Markham, Ontario, Canada L3R 1B4
Penguin Books (NZ) Ltd, 182–190 Wairau Road, Auckland 10, New Zealand

Penguin Books Ltd, Registered Offices: Harmondsworth, Middlesex, England

First published 1989
10 9 8 7 6 5 4 3 2 1

Pictures copyright © Gordon Beningfield, 1978, 1980, 1983, 1985, 1987, 1988, 1989
Design copyright © Cameron Books, 1989

Selected and designed by Jill Hollis and Ian Cameron

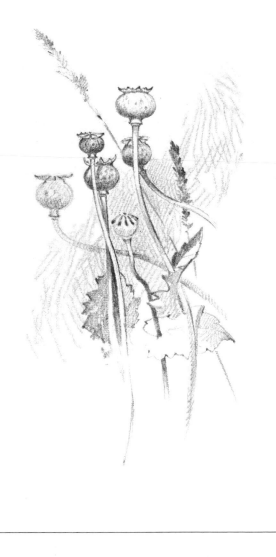

Filmset in Linotype Baskerville by Cameron Books
Printed in The Netherlands by Royal Smeets Offset, Weert

A CIP catalogue record for this book is available from the British Library

ISBN 0-670-83035-6

For permission to reprint some of the poems included in this book we thank the
following:
'The Dandelion' by Richard Church, The Estate of Richard Church; 'Bee! I'm
expecting you' by Emily Dickinson from *The Poems of Emily Dickinson* edited by Thomas
H. Johnson copyright 1951, © 1955, 1979, 1983 by the President and Fellows of
Harvard College, The Belknap Press of Harvard University Press and the Trustees of
Amherst College; 'For Samuel Palmer' by Gavin Ewart, Century Hutchinson; 'Fox'
and 'A Swallow' by Ted Hughes, 'Going, Going' and 'The Trees' by Philip Larkin, and
'Dandelions' by Louis MacNeice, Faber and Faber Ltd; 'Cloud' and 'Wind' by
Kathleen Raine, Unwin Hyman Ltd; 'The Nest', 'The Snail' and 'The Swallows' by
Andrew Young, Martin Secker & Warburg Ltd; 'Flying Crooked' by Robert Graves,
A.P. Watt Ltd on behalf of the Executors of the Estate of Robert Graves; 'Conservation
Piece' by Roger McGough, Peters Fraser & Dunlop Group Ltd; 'Another Spring' by
Siegfried Sassoon, George T. Sassoon.

Pictures

Poems

The Soldier

If I should die, think only this of me:
That there's some corner of a foreign field
That is for ever England. There shall be
In that rich earth a richer dust concealed;
A dust whom England bore, shaped, made aware,
Gave, once, her flowers to love, her ways to roam,
A body of England's, breathing English air,
Washed by the rivers, blest by suns of home.

And think, this heart, all evil shed away,
A pulse in the eternal mind, no less
Gives somewhere back the thoughts by England given;
Her sights and sounds; dreams happy as her day;
And laughter, learnt of friends; and gentleness,
In hearts at peace, under an English heaven.

RUPERT BROOKE (1887-1915)

Song in Absence

Green fields of England! wheresoe'er
Across this watery waste we fare,
Your image at our hearts we bear,
Green fields of England, everywhere.

Sweet eyes in England, I must flee
Past where the waves' last confines be,
Ere your loved smile I cease to see,
Sweet eyes in England, dear to me!

Dear home in England, safe and fast
If but in thee my lot lie cast,
The past shall seem a nothing past
To thee, dear home, if won at last;
Dear home in England, won at last.

ARTHUR HUGH CLOUGH (1819-1861)

England

Into my heart an air that kills
From yon far country blows:
What are those blue remember'd hills,
What spires, what farms are those?

That is the land of lost content,
I see it shining plain,
The happy highways where I went
And cannot come again.

A.E. HOUSMAN (1859-1936)

Jerusalem

And did those feet in ancient time
Walk upon England's mountain green?
And was the holy Lamb of God
On England's pleasant pastures seen?

And did the countenance divine
Shine forth upon our clouded hills?
And was Jerusalem builded here
Among these dark Satanic mills?

Bring me my bow of burning gold!
Bring me my arrows of desire!
Bring me my spear: O clouds, unfold!
Bring me my chariot of fire!

I will not cease from mental fight,
Nor shall my sword sleep in my hand,
Till we have built Jerusalem
In England's green and pleasant land.

WILLIAM BLAKE (1757-1827)

Early Spring
from *In Memoriam*

Now fades the last long streak of snow,
Now burgeons every maze of quick
About the flowering squares, and thick
By ashen roots the violets blow.

Now rings the woodland loud and long,
The distance takes a lovelier hue,
And drowned in yonder living blue
The lark becomes a sightless song.

Now dance the lights on lawn and lea,
The flocks are whiter down the vale,
And milkier every milky sail
On winding stream or distant sea;

Where now the seamew pipes, or dives
In yonder greening gleam, and fly
The happy birds, that change their sky
To build and brood; that live their lives

From land to land; and in my breast
Spring wakens too; and my regret
Becomes an April violet,
And buds and blossoms like the rest.

ALFRED, LORD TENNYSON (1809-1892)

Written in Early Spring

I heard a thousand blended notes
While in a grove I sate reclined,
In that sweet mood when pleasant thoughts
Bring sad thoughts to the mind.

To her fair works did Nature link
The human soul that through me ran;
And much it grieved my heart to think
What Man has made of Man.

Through primrose tufts, in that sweet bower,
The periwinkle trail'd its wreaths;
And 'tis my faith that every flower
Enjoys the air it breathes.

The birds around me hopp'd and play'd,
Their thoughts I cannot measure, –
But the least motion which they made
It seem'd a thrill of pleasure.

The budding twigs spread out their fan
To catch the breezy air;
And I must think, do all I can,
That there was pleasure there.

If this belief from heaven be sent,
If such be Nature's holy plan,
Have I not reason to lament
What Man has made of Man?

WILLIAM WORDSWORTH (1770-1850)

Another Spring

Aged self, disposed to lose his hold on life,
Looks down, at winter's evening, and perceives
Continuance in some crinkled primrose leaves.
A noise of nesting rooks in tangled trees.
Stillness – inbreathed, expectant. Shadows that bring
Cloud-castled thoughts from downland distances.
Eyes, ears are old. But not the sense of spring.

Look, listen, live, some inward watcher warns.
Absorb his moment's meaning: and be wise
With hearts whom the first primrose purifies.

SIEGFRIED SASSOON (1886-1967)

17

Spring

Nothing is so beautiful as Spring –
When weeds, in wheels, shoot long and lovely and lush;
Thrush's eggs look little low heavens, and thrush
Through the echoing timber does so rinse and wring

The ear, it strikes like lightnings to hear him sing;
The glassy peartree leaves and blooms, they brush
The descending blue; that blue is all in a rush
With richness; the racing lambs too have fair their fling.

What is all this juice and all this joy?
A strain of the earth's sweet being in the beginning
In Eden garden. – Have, get, before it cloy,

Before it cloud, Christ, lord, and sour with sinning,
Innocent mind and Mayday in girl and boy,
Most, O maid's child, thy choice and worthy the winning.

GERARD MANLEY HOPKINS (1844-1889)

Spring

The rarer pleasure is, it is more sweet,
And friends are kindest when they seldom meet.
Who would not hear the nightingale still sing,
Or who grew ever weary of the spring?
The day must have her night, the spring her fall,
All is divided, none is lord of all.
It were a most delightful thing,
To live in a perpetual spring.

ANONYMOUS

The Nest

Four blue stones in this thrush's nest
I leave, content to make the best
Of turquoise, lapis lazuli
Or for that matter of the whole blue sky.

ANDREW YOUNG (1885-1971)

The Thrush's Nest

Within a thick and spreading hawthorn bush
That overhung a mole-hill large and round,
I heard from morn to morn a merry thrush
Sing hymns to sunrise, and I drank the sound
With joy; and, often an intruding guest,
I watched her secret toils from day to day –
How true she warped the moss to form a nest,
And modelled it within the wood and clay;
And by and by, like heath-bells gilt with dew,
There lay her shining eggs, as bright as flowers,
Ink-spotted over shells of greeny blue;
And there I witnessed, in the sunny hours,
A brood of nature's minstrels chirp and fly,
Glad as that sunshine and the laughing sky.

JOHN CLARE (1793-1864)

The Wren

Why is the cuckoo's melody preferred,
And nightingale's rich songs so madly praised
In poets' rhymes? Is there no other bird
Of nature's minstrelsy, that oft hath raised
One's heart to ecstasy and mirth as well?
I judge not how another's taste is caught,
With mine are other birds that bear the bell,
Whose song hath crowds of happy memories brought:
Such the wood robin, singing in the dell,
And little wren, that many a time hath sought
Shelter from showers, in huts where I did dwell
In early spring, the tenant of the plain,
Tenting my sheep; and still they come to tell
The happy stories of the past again.

JOHN CLARE (1793-1864)

from *The Eternity of Nature*

All nature's ways are mysteries! Endless youth
Lives in them all, unchangeable as truth.
With the odd number five, her curious laws
Play many freaks, nor once mistake the cause;
For in the cowslip-peeps this very day
Five spots appear, which Time wears not away,
Nor once mistakes in counting – look within
Each peep, and five, nor more nor less, are seen.
So trailing bindweed, with its pinky cup,
Five leaves of paler hue go streaking up;
And many a bird, too, keeps the rule alive,
Laying five eggs, nor more nor less than five.
But flowers, how many own that mystic power,
With five leaves ever making up the flower!
The five-leaved grass, mantling its golden cup
Of flowers – five leaves make all for which I stoop.
The bryony, in the hedge, that now adorns
The tree to which it clings, and now the thorns,
Owns five-starred pointed leaves of dingy white;
Count which I will, all make the number right.
The spreading goose-grass, trailing all abroad
In leaves of silver green about the road –
Five leaves make every blossom all along.
I stoop for many, none are counted wrong.
'Tis Nature's wonder, and her Maker's will,
Who bade earth be, and order owns him still,
As that superior Power, who keeps the key
Of wisdom and of might through all eternity.

JOHN CLARE (1793-1864)

Tewkesbury Road

It is good to be out on the road, and going one knows not where,
Going through meadow and village, one knows not whither nor why;
Through the grey light drift of the dust, in the keen cool rush of the air,
Under the flying white clouds, and the broad blue lift of the sky;

And to halt at the chattering brook, in the tall green fern at the brink
Where the harebell grows, and the gorse, and the fox-gloves purple and white;
Where the shy-eyed delicate deer troop down to the pools to drink,
When the stars are mellow and large at the coming on of the night.

O! to feel the warmth of the rain, and the homely smell of the earth,
Is a tune for the blood to jig to, a joy past power of words;
And the blessed green comely meadows seem all a-ripple with mirth
At the lilt of the shifting feet, and the dear wild cry of the birds.

JOHN MASEFIELD (1878-1967)

A Spring Morning

The Spring comes in with all her hues and smells,
In freshness breathing over hills and dells;
O'er woods where May her gorgeous drapery flings,
And meads washed fragrant by their laughing springs.
Fresh are new opened flowers, untouched and free
From the bold rifling of the amorous bee.
The happy time of singing birds is come,
And Love's lone pilgrimage now finds a home;
Among the mossy oaks now coos the dove,
And the hoarse crow finds softer notes for love.
The foxes play around their dens, and bark
In joy's excess, 'mid woodland shadows dark.
The flowers join lips below; the leaves above;
And every sound that meets the ear is Love.

JOHN CLARE (1793-1864)

Song on May Morning

Now the bright morning Star, Days harbinger,
Comes dancing from the East, and leads with her
The Flowry *May*, who from her green lap throws
The yellow Cowslip and the pale Primrose.
Hail, bounteous *May* that dost inspire
Mirth and youth and warm desire
Woods and Groves are of thy dressing,
Hill and Dale doth boast thy blessing.
Thus we salute thee with our early Song,
And welcom thee, and wish thee long.

JOHN MILTON (1608-1674)

Spring Goeth All in White

Spring goeth all in white,
Crowned with milk-white may:
In fleecy flocks of light
O'er heaven the white clouds stray:

White butterflies in the air;
White daisies prank the ground:
The cherry and hoary pear
Scatter their snow around.

ROBERT BRIDGES (1844-1930)

I Bended Unto Me

I bended unto me a bough of may,
That I might see and smell:
It bore it in a sort of way,
It bore it very well.
But when I let it backward sway,
Then it were hard to tell
With what a toss, with what a swing,
The dainty thing
Resumed its proper level,
And sent me to the devil.
I know it did – you doubt it?
I turned, and saw them whispering about it.

T.E. BROWN (1830-1897)

Lovely May
from *Milton*

. . . the White-thorn, lovely May,
Opens her many lovely eyes listening; the Rose still sleeps,
None dare to wake her; soon she bursts her crimson-curtain'd bed
And comes forth in the majesty of beauty . . .

WILLIAM BLAKE (1757-1827)

from *Fidelity*

O flowers they fade because they are moving swiftly; a little torrent of life
leaps up to the summit of the stem, gleams, turns over round the bend
of the parabola of curved flight,
sinks, and is gone, like a comet curving into the invisible.

O flowers they are all the time travelling
like comets, and they come into our ken
for a day, for two days, and withdraw, slowly vanish again.

And we, we must take them on the wing, and let them go.
Embalmed flowers are not flowers, immortelles are not flowers;
flowers are just a motion, a swift motion, a coloured gesture;
that is their loveliness. And that is love.

D.H. LAWRENCE (1885-1930)

The Unknown Bird

Three lovely notes he whistled, too soft to be heard
If others sang; but others never sang
In the great beech-wood all that May and June.
No one saw him: I alone could hear him
Though many listened. Was it but four years
Ago? or five? He never came again.

Oftenest when I heard him I was alone,
Nor could I ever make another hear.
La-la-la! he called seeming far-off –
As if a cock crowed past the edge of the world,
As if the bird or I were in a dream.
Yet that he travelled through the trees and sometimes
Neared me, was plain, though somehow distant still
He sounded. All the proof is – I told men
What I had heard.

I never knew a voice,
Man, beast, or bird, better than this. I told
The naturalists; but neither had they heard
Anything like the notes that did so haunt me,
I had them clear by heart and have them still.
Four years, or five, have made no difference. Then
As now that La-la-la! was bodiless sweet:
Sad more than joyful it was, if I must say
That it was one or other, but if sad
'Twas sad only with joy too, too far off
For me to taste it. But I cannot tell
If truly never anything but fair
The days were when he sang, as now they seem.
This surely I know, that I who listened then,
Happy sometimes, sometimes suffering
A heavy body and a heavy heart,
Now straightway, if I think of it, become
Light as that bird wandering beyond my shore.

EDWARD THOMAS (1878-1917)

from *The Bluebells*

We stood upon the grass beside the road,
At a wood's fence, to look among the trees.
In windless noon the burning May-time glowed.
Gray, in young green, the beeches stood at ease.
Light speckled in the wood or left it dim:
There lay a blue in which no ship could swim,
Within whose peace no water ever flowed.

Within that pool no shadow ever showed:
Tideless was all that mystery of blue.
Out of eternities man never knew
A living growth man never reaped or sowed
Snatched in the dim its fitness from the hour
A miracle unspeakable of flower
That tears in the heart's anguish answered to.

How paint it; how describe? None has the power.
It only had the power upon the soul
To consecrate the spirit and the hour,
To light to sudden rapture and console,
Its beauty called a truce: forgave: forgot
All the long horror of man's earthly lot,
A miracle unspeakable of flower
In a green May unutterably blue.

JOHN MASEFIELD (1878-1967)

The Dandelion

I am the sun's remembrancer, the boy
Who runs in hedgerow, and in field and garden,
Showing his badge, a round-faced golden joy
With tips of flame. I bear my master's pardon
For my long, greedy roots. I bring his message
And pay his sovereign coin for my passage.
If any call me robber of the soil,
Let him but wait on windy weather, note
How easily, without a mortal's toil,
I change my gold to silver treasure, float
The fairy mintage on the air, and then
Defy the curse of all industrious men.

RICHARD CHURCH (1893-1972)

Dandelions
from *Nature Notes*

Incorrigible, brash,
They brightened the cinder path of my childhood,
Unsubtle, the opposite of primroses,
But, unlike primroses, capable
Of growing anywhere, railway track, pierhead,
Like our extrovert friends who never
Make us fall in love, yet fill
The primroseless roseless gaps.

LOUIS MACNEICE (1907-1963)

The First Dandelion

Simple and fresh and fair from winter's close emerging,
Forth from its sunny nook of sheltered grass – innocent,
   golden, calm as the dawn,
The spring's first dandelion shows its trustful face.

WALT WHITMAN (1819-1892)

The Dandelion

With locks of gold to-day;
To-morrow, silver grey;
Then blossom-bald. Behold,
O man, they fortune told!

JOHN B. TABB (19th century)

The Tree

Fair *Tree*! for thy delightful Shade
'Tis just that some Return be made:
Sure, some Return is due from me
To thy cool Shadows, and to thee.
When thou to *Birds* do'st Shelter give,
Thou Musick do'st from them receive;
If Travellers beneath thee stay,
'Till Storms have worn themselves away,
That Time in praising thee they spend,
And thy protecting Pow'r commend:
The *Shepherd* here, from Scorching freed,
Tunes to thy dancing Leaves his Reed;
Whilst his lov'd Nymph, in Thanks, bestows
Her flow'ry Chaplets on thy Boughs.
Shall I then only Silent be,
And no Return be made by me?

No; let this Wish upon thee wait,
And still to flourish be thy Fate,
To future Ages may'st thou stand
Untouch'd by the rash Workman's hand;
'Till that large Stock of Sap is spent,
Which gives thy Summer's Ornament;
'Till the fierce Winds, that vainly strive
To shock thy Greatness whilst alive,
Shall on thy lifeless Hour attend,
Prevent the Axe, and grace thy End;
Their scatter'd Strength together call,
And to the Clouds proclaim thy Fall;
Who then their Ev'ning-Dews may spare,
When thou no longer art their Care;
But shalt, like ancient Heroes, burn,
And some bright Hearth be made thy Urn.

ANNE FINCH, COUNTESS OF WINCHILSEA (1661-1720)

The Trees

The trees are coming into leaf
Like something almost being said;
The recent buds relax and spread,
Their greenness is a kind of grief.

Is it that they are born again
And we grow old? No, they die too.
Their yearly trick of looking new
Is written down in rings of grain.

Yet still the unresting castles thresh
In fullgrown thickness every May.
Last year is dead, they seem to say,
Begin afresh, afresh, afresh.

PHILIP LARKIN (1922-1985)

The Butterfly

He the gay garden round about doth fly,
From bed to bed, from one to other border,
And takes survey with curious busy eye
Of every flower and herb there set in order;
Now this, now that, he tasteth tenderly,
Ye none of them he rudely doth disorder,
Ne with his feet their silken leaves deface,
But pastures on the pleasures of each place,

And evermore with most variety
And change of sweetness (for all change is sweet),
He casts his glutton sense to gratify;
Now sucking of the sap of herb most meet,
Or of the dew which yet on them does lie,
Now in the same bathing his tender feet;
And then he percheth on some branch thereby
To weather him, and his moist wings to dry.

EDMUND SPENSER (1552 or 1553-1599)

Flowers

Yes; there is heaven about you: in your breath
And hues it dwells. The stars of heaven ye shine;
Bright strangers in a land of sin and death,
That talk of God, and point to realms divine . . .

Ye speak of frail humanity: ye tell
How man, like you, shall flourish and shall fall: –
But ah! ye speak of Heavenly Love as well,
And say, the God of flowers is God of all . . .

Sweet flowers, sweet flowers! the rich exuberance
Of Nature's heart in her propitious hours:
When glad emotions in her bosom dance
She vents her happiness in laughing flowers . . .

Childhood and you are playmates; matching well
Your sunny cheeks, and mingling fragrant breath: –
Ye help young Love his faltering tale to tell;
Ye scatter sweetness o'er the bed of Death.

HENRY FRANCIS LYTE (1793-1847)

Rag-wort

Nobody considers rag-wort a flower.
It comes too late, and in wrong places.
Some say it stinks of rotten apples
And sours the ground it grows upon.
But I have watched for many an hour
The pattern a colony of it traces
Along a river's bank, the sun
Spilled over it and gilding the ripples
When no other colour can be seen
But green, mile after mile of green.

In the minority, I'll concede
To those who hold it in disdain,
That rag-wort is a rebel weed
And should be rooted out, or ploughed
Under, never to be seen again.
But still, in memory, a cloud
Of meadow butterflies will hover
Where that untidy blossom shook
Gold-dust into the passing brook.
Only those ephemeral wings
Will grieve; and perhaps one who sings.

RICHARD CHURCH (1893-1972)

Flying Crooked

The butterfly, a cabbage-white,
(His honest idiocy of flight)
Will never now, it is too late,
Master the art of flying straight,
Yet has – who knows so well as I? –
A just sense of how not to fly:
He lurches here and here by guess
And God and hope and hopelessness.
Even the aerobatic swift
Has not his flying-crooked gift.

ROBERT GRAVES (1895-1985)

from *Thoughts in a Garden*

And, as it works, th' industrious bee
Computes its time as well as we.
How could such sweet and wholesome hours
Be reckoned, but with herbs and flowers!

ANDREW MARVELL (1621-1678)

'Bee! I'm expecting you!'

Bee! I'm expecting you!
Was saying Yesterday
To Somebody you know
That you were due –

The Frogs got Home last Week –
Are settled, and at work –
Birds, mostly back –
The Clover warm and thick –

You'll get my Letter by
The seventeenth; Reply
Or better, be with me –
Yours, Fly.

EMILY DICKINSON (1830-1886)

To a Butterfly

I've watched you now a full half-hour,
Self-poised upon that yellow flower;
And, little Butterfly! indeed
I know not if you sleep or feed,
How motionless! – not frozen seas
More motionless! and then
What joy awaits you, when the breeze
Hath found you out among the trees,
And calls you forth again!

This plot of Orchard-ground is ours;
My trees they are, my Sister's flowers;
Here rest your wings when they are weary;
Here lodge as in a sanctuary!
Come often to us, fear no wrong;
Sit near us on the bough!
We'll talk of sunshine and of song,
And summer days, when we were young;
Sweet childish days, that were as long
As twenty days are now.

WILLIAM WORDSWORTH (1770-1850)

The Swallows

All day – when early morning shone
With every dewdrop its own dawn
And when cockchafers were abroad
Hurtling like missiles that had lost their road –

The swallows twisting here and there
Round unseen corners of the air
Upstream and down so quickly passed
I wondered that their shadows flew as fast.

They steeplechased over the bridge
And dropped down to a drowning midge
Sharing the river with the fish,
Although the air itself was their chief dish.

Blue-winged snowballs! until they turned
And then with ruddy breasts they burned;
All in one instant everywhere,
Jugglers with their own bodies in the air.

ANDREW YOUNG (1885-1971)

The Faithful Swallow

When summer shone
Its sweetest on
An August day,
'Here evermore,'
I said, 'I'll stay;
Not go away
To another shore
As fickle they!'

December came:
'Twas not the same!
I did not know
Fidelity
Would serve me so.
Frost, hunger, snow;
And now, ah me,
Too late to go!

THOMAS HARDY (1840-1928)

A Swallow

Has slipped through a fracture in the snow-sheet
Which is still our sky —

She flicks past, ahead of her name,
Twinkling away out over the lake.

Reaching this way and that way, with her scissors,
Snipping midges
Trout are still too numb and sunken to stir for.

Sahara clay ovens, at mirage heat,
Glazed her blues, and still she is hot.

She wearied of snatching clegs off the lugs of buffaloes
And of lassooing the flirt-flags of gazelles.

They told her the North was one giant snowball
Rolling South. She did not believe them.
So she exchanged the starry chart of Columbus
For a beggar's bowl of mud.

Setting her compass-tremor tail-needles
She harpooned a wind
That wallowed in the ocean,
Working her barbs deeper
Through that twisting mass she came —

Did she close her eyes and trust in God?
No, she saw lighthouses
Streaming in chaos
Like sparks from a chimney —

She had fixed her instruments on home.

And now, suddenly, into a blanch-tree stillness
A silence of celandines,
A fringing and stupor of frost
She bursts, weightless —
                                    to anchor
On eggs frail as frost.

There she goes, flung taut on her leash,
Her eyes at her mouth-corners,
Water-skiing out across a wind
That wrecks great flakes against windscreens.

TED HUGHES (b 1930)

The Best Thing in the World

What's the best thing in the world?
June-rose, by May-dew impearled;
Sweet south-wind, that means no rain;
Truth, not cruel to a friend;
Pleasure, not in haste to end;
Beauty, not self-decked and curled
Till its pride is over-plain;
Light, that never makes you wink;
Memory, that gives no pain;
Love, when, *so*, you're loved again.
What's the best thing in the world?
– Something out of it, I think.

ELIZABETH BARRETT BROWNING (1806-1861)

The Rose

Thou blushing Rose, within whose virgin leaves
The wanton wind to sport himself presumes,
Whilst from their rifled wardrobe he receives
For his wings purple, for his breath perfumes:
Blown in the morning, thou shalt fade ere noon;
What boots a life which in such haste forsakes thee!
Thou'rt wondrous frolic, being to die so soon,
And passing proud a little colour makes thee.

SIR RICHARD FANSHAWE (1608-1666)

The Wild Rose and the Snowdrop

The Snowdrop is the prophet of the flowers;
It lives and dies upon its bed of snows;
And like a thought of spring it comes and goes,
Hanging its head beside our leafless bowers.
The sun's betrothing kiss it never knows,
Nor all the glowing joy of golden showers;
But ever in a placid, pure repose,
More like a spirit with its look serene,
Droops its pale cheek veined thro' with infant green.

Queen of her sisters is the sweet Wild Rose,
Sprung from the earnest sun and ripe young June;
The year's own darling and the Summer's Queen!
Lustrous as the new-throned crescent moon.
Much of that early prophet look she shows,
Mixed with her fair espoused blush which glows,
As if the ethereal fairy blood were seen;
Like a soft evening over sunset snows,
Half twilight violet shade, half crimson sheen.

Twin-born are both in beauteousness, most fair
In all that glads the eye and charms the air;
In all that wakes emotions in the mind
And sows sweet sympathies for human kind.
Twin-born, albeit their seasons are apart,
They bloom together in the thoughtful heart;
Fair symbols of the marvels of our state,
Mute speakers of the oracles of fate!
For each, fulfilling nature's law, fulfils

Itself and its own aspirations pure;
Living and dying; letting faith ensure
New life when deathless spring shall touch the hills.
Each perfect in its place; and each content
With that perfection which its being meant:
Divided not by months that intervene,
But linked by all the flowers that bud between.
Forever smiling thro' its season brief,
The one in glory and the one in grief:
Forever painting to our museful sight,
How lowlihead and loveliness unite.

Born from the first blind yearning of the earth
To be a mother and give happy birth,
Ere yet the northern sun such rapture brings,
Lo, from her virgin breast the Snowdrop springs;
And ere the snows have melted from the grass,
And not a strip of greensward doth appear,
Save the faint prophecy its cheeks declare,
Alone, unkissed, unloved, behold it pass!
While in the ripe enthronement of the year,
Whispering the breeze, and wedding the rich air
With her so sweet, delicious bridal breath, –
Odorous and exquisite beyond compare,
And starr'd with dews upon her forehead clear,
Fresh-hearted as a Maiden Queen should be
Who takes the land's devotion as her fee, –
The Wild Rose blooms, all summer for her dower,
Nature's most beautiful and perfect flower.

GEORGE MEREDITH (1828-1909)

The Dell

A green and silent spot amid the hills,
A small and silent dell! O'er stiller place
No singing sky-lark ever poised himself.
The hills are heathy, save that swelling slope
Which hath a gay and gorgeous covering on,
All golden with the never-bloomless furze,
Which now blooms most profusely: but the dell
Bathed by the mist is fresh and delicate
As vernal corn-field, or the unripe flax,
When through its half-transparent stalks at eve
The level sunshine glimmers with green light.

SAMUEL TAYLOR COLERIDGE (1772-1834)

The Old Country

O England, country of my heart's desire,
Land of the hedgerow and the village spire,
Land of thatched cottages and murmuring bees,
And wayside inns where one may take one's ease,
Of village greens where cricket may be played,
And fat old spaniels sleeping in the shade. –
O homeland, far away across the main,
How would I love to see your face again! –
Your daisied meadows and your grassy hills,
Your primrose banks, your parks, your tinkling rills,
Your copses where the purple bluebells grow,
Your quiet lanes where lovers loiter so,
Your cottage-gardens with their wallflowers' scent,
Your swallows 'neath the eaves, your sweet content!
And 'mid the fleecy clouds that o'er you spread,
Listen, the skylark singing overhead . . .
That's the old country, that's the old home!
You never forget it wherever you roam.

E.V. LUCAS (1868-1938)

A Thing of Beauty is a Joy For Ever

A thing of beauty is a joy for ever:
Its loveliness increases; it will never
Pass into nothingness; but still will keep
A bower quiet for us, and a sleep
Full of sweet dreams, and health, and quiet breathing.
Therefore, on every morrow, are we wreathing
A flowery band to bind us to the earth,
Spite of despondence, of the inhuman dearth
Of noble natures, of the gloomy days,
Of all the unhealthy and o'er-darken'd ways
Made for our searching: yes, in spite of all,
Some shape of beauty moves away the pall
From our dark spirits. Such the sun, the moon,
Trees old and young, sprouting a shady boon
For simple sheep; and such are daffodils
With the green world they live in; and clear rills
That for themselves a cooling covert make
'Gainst the hot season; the mid-forest brake,
Rich with a sprinkling of fair musk-rose blooms:
And such too is the grandeur of the dooms
We have imagined for the mighty dead;
All lovely tales that we have heard or read:
An endless fountain of immortal drink,
Pouring unto us from the heaven's brink.

Nor do we merely feel these essences
For one short hour; no, even as the trees
That whisper round a temple become soon
Dear as the temple's self, so does the moon,
The passion poesy, glories infinite,
Haunt us till they become a cheering light
Unto our souls, and bound to us so fast,
That, whether there be shine, or gloom o'ercast,
They alway must be with us, or we die. . . .

JOHN KEATS (1795-1821)

The Beauty of England

I learnt to love that England. Very oft,
Before the day was born, or otherwise
Through secret windings of the afternoons,
I threw my hunters off and plunged myself
Among the deep hills, as a hunted stag
Will take the waters, shivering with the fear
And passion of the course. And when, at last
Escaped, – so many a green slope built on slope
Betwixt me and the enemy's house behind,
I dared to rest, or wander, – in a rest
Made sweeter for the step upon the grass, –
And view the ground's most gentle dimplement,
(As if God's finger touched, but did not press
In making England!), such an up and down
Of verdure, – nothing too much up or down,
A ripple of land; such little hills, the sky
Can stoop too tenderly and the wheatfields climb;
Such nooks of valleys, lined with orchises,
Fed full of noises by invisible streams;
And open pastures, where you scarcely tell
White daisies from white dew, – at intervals
The mythic oaks and elm-trees standing out
Self-posed upon their prodigy of shade, –
I thought my father's land was worthy too
Of being my Shakespeare's.

I flattered all the beauteous country round
As poets use, the skies, the clouds, the fields,
The happy violets hiding from the roads
The primroses run down to, carrying gold;
The tangled hedgerows, where the cows push out
Impatient horns and tolerant churning mouths
'Twixt dripping ash-boughs, – hedgerows all alive
With birds and gnats and large white butterflies
Which look as if the May-flower had caught life
And palpitated forth upon the wind, –
Hills, vales, woods, netted in a silver mist,
Farms, granges, doubled up among the hills,
And cattle grazing in the watered vales,
And cottage-chimneys smoking from the woods,
And cottage-gardens smelling everywhere,
Confused with smell of orchards. 'See,' I said,
'And see! is God not with us on the earth?
And shall we put Him down by aught we do?
Who says there's nothing for the poor and vile
Save poverty and wickedness? behold!'
And ankle-deep in English grass I leaped
And clapped my hands, and called all very fair.

ELIZABETH BARRETT BROWNING (1806-1861)

Britannia

Heavens! what a goodly prospect spreads around,
Of hills, and dales, and woods, and lawns, and spires,
And glittering towns, and gilded streams, till all
The stretching landscape into smoke decays!
Happy Britannia! where, the Queen of Arts
Inspiring vigour, liberty abroad
Walks, unconfined, e'en to thy farthest cots,
And scatters plenty with unsparing hand.
Rich is thy soil, and merciful thy clime;
Thy streams unfailing in the summer's drought;
Unmatched thy guardian oaks; thy valleys float
With golden waves: and, on thy mountains flocks
Bleat numberless; while, roving round their sides,
Bellow the blackening herds in lusty droves.
Beneath, thy meadows glow, and rise unquelled
Against the mower's scythe. On every hand
Thy villas shine. Thy country teems with wealth;
And property assures it to the swain,
Pleased and unwearied, in his guarded toil.

JAMES THOMSON (1700-1748)

from *Richard II*

This royal throne of kings, this sceptered isle,
This earth of majesty, this seat of Mars,
This other Eden, demi-paradise;
This fortress built by Nature for herself
Against infection and the hand of war;
This happy breed of men, this little world;
This precious stone set in the silver sea,
Which serves it in the office of a wall,
Or as a moat defensive to a house,
Against the envy of less happier lands;
This blessed plot, this earth, this realm, this England . . .

WILLIAM SHAKESPEARE (1564-1616)

To a Skylark

Hail to thee, blithe spirit!
Bird thou never wert –
That from heaven or near it
Pourest thy full heart
In profuse strains of unpremeditated art.

Higher still and higher
From the earth thou springest,
Like a cloud of fire;
The blue deep thou wingest,
And singing still dost soar, and soaring ever singest.

In the golden light'ning
Of the sunken sun,
O'er which clouds are bright'ning,
Thou dost float and run,
Like an unbodied joy whose race is just begun.

The pale purple even
Melts around thy flight;
Like a star of heaven,
In the broad daylight
Thou art unseen, but yet I hear thy shrill delight –

Keen as are the arrows
Of that silver sphere
Whose intense lamp narrows
In the white dawn clear,
Until we hardly see, we feel that it is there.

All the earth and air
With thy voice is loud
As, when night is bare,
From one lonely cloud
The moon rains out her beams, and heaven is overflow'd.

What thou art we know not;
What is most like thee?
From rainbow clouds there flow not
Drops so bright to see,
As from thy presence showers a rain of melody:-

Like a poet hidden
In the light of thought,
Singing hymns unbidden,
Till the world is wrought
To sympathy with hopes and fears it heeded not:

Like a high-born maiden
In a palace tower,
Soothing her love-laden
Soul in secret hour
With music sweet as love, which overflows her bower:

Like a glow-worm golden
In a dell of dew,
Scattering unbeholden
Its aërial hue
Among the flowers and grass which screen it from the view:

Like a rose embower'd
In its own green leaves,
By warm winds deflower'd,
Till the scent it gives
Makes faint with too much sweet these heavy-wingèd thieves:

Sound of vernal showers
On the twinkling grass,
Rain-awaken'd flowers –
All that ever was
Joyous and clear and fresh – thy music doth surpass.

Teach us, sprite or bird,
What sweet thoughts are thine:
I have never heard
Praise of love or wine
That panted forth a flood of rapture so divine.

Chorus hymeneal,
Or triumphal chant,
Match'd with thine would be all
But an empty vaunt –
A thing wherein we feel there is some hidden want.

What objects are the fountains
Of thy happy strain?
What fields, or waves, or mountains?
What shapes of sky or plain?
What love of thine own kind? what ignorance of pain?

With thy clear keen joyance
Languor cannot be:
Shadow of annoyance
Never came near thee:
Thou lovest, but ne'er knew love's sad satiety.

Waking or asleep,
Thou of death must deem
Things more true and deep
Than we mortals dream,
Or how could thy notes flow in such a crystal stream?

We look before and after,
And pine for what is not:
Our sincerest laughter
With some pain is fraught;
Our sweetest songs are those that tell of saddest thought.

Yet, if we could scorn
Hate and pride and fear,
If we were things born
Not to shed a tear,
I know not how thy joy we ever should come near.

Better than all measures
Of delightful sound,
Better than all treasures
That in books are found,
Thy skill to poet were, thou scorner of the ground!

Teach me half the gladness
That thy brain must know;
Such harmonious madness
From my lips would flow,
The world should listen then, as I am listening now.

PERCY BYSSHE SHELLEY (1792-1822)

The Skylark

Bird of the wilderness,
Blithesome and cumberless,
Sweet by thy matin o'er moorland and lea!
Emblem of happiness,
Blest is thy dwelling-place –
O to abide in the desert with thee!
Wild is thy lay and loud,
Far in the downy cloud,
Love gives it energy, love gave it birth.
Where, on thy dewy wing,
Where art thou journeying?
Thy lay is in heaven, thy love is on earth.

O'er fell and fountain sheen,
O'er moor and mountain green,
O'er the red streamer that heralds the day,
Over the cloudlet dim,
Over the rainbow's rim,
Musical cherub, soar, singing, away!
Then, when the gloaming comes,
Low in the heather blooms
Sweet will thy welcome and bed of love be!
Emblem of happiness,
Blest is thy dwelling-place –
O to abide in the desert with thee!

JAMES HOGG (1770-1835)

from *The Lark*

The giddy lark reacheth the steepy air
By sweet degrees, making each note a stair.
Her voice leads softly on, the feathered strain
Follows and leaves the last note to her train.
At the first stage she rests, seeming to tire;
Her wing mounts up her voice some eight notes higher.
At the next period in this airy hill,
Her rising voice lifts up her restive quill.
Hard tale to tell, when she her matins sings,
Whether her tongue gives, or receives her wings.
To the observing ear, attentive eye,
Her wings would seem to chant, her tongue to fly.
Brave flight of music, and a sublime song,
When wings thus sweetly fly into a tongue!

ANONYMOUS (17th century)

Up on the Downs

Up on the downs the red-eyed kestrels hover,
Eyeing the grass.
The field-mouse flits like a shadow into cover
As their shadows pass.

Men are burning the gorse on the down's shoulder;
A drift of smoke
Glitters with fire and hangs, and the skies smoulder,
And the lungs choke.

Once the tribe did thus on the down, on these downs burning
Men in the frame,
Crying to the gods of the downs till their brains were turning
And the gods came.

And to-day on the downs, in the wind, the hawks, the grasses,
In blood and air,
Something passes me and cries as it passes,
On the chalk downland bare.

JOHN MASEFIELD (1878-1967)

Wind

Companionless,
Without trace you are,
Without identity,
Without person or place,
Without name or destination,
Unbeginning, unending, unresting,
Are but speed and motion,
Crying without voice,
Without memory lamenting,
Without grief moaning, without anger storming,
Singing without joy, whistling to no-one:
Signifying nothing wind
You are yet of my kind,
Habitant of the same hills,
Wanderer over the same waters,
Beater against cliff-face,
We are the one world's way,
Move in the universal courses;
You blow over,
Breath through me always.

KATHLEEN RAINE (1935-1980)

Summer Wind

It is a sultry day; the sun has drunk
The dew that lay upon the morning grass;
There is no rustling in the lofty elm
That canopies my dwelling, and its shade
Scarce cools me. All is silent, save the faint
And interrupted murmur of the bee,
Settling on the sick flowers, and then again
Instantly on the wing. The plants around
Feel the too potent fervors: the tall maize
Rolls up its long green leaves; the clover droops
Its tender foliage, and declines its blooms.
But far in the fierce sunshine tower the hills,
With all their growth of woods, silent and stern,
As if the scorching heat and dazzling light
Were but an element they loved. Bright clouds,
Motionless pillars of the brazen heaven –
Their bases on the mountains – their white tops
Shining in the far ether – fire the air
With a reflected radiance, and make turn
The gazer's eye away. For me, I lie
Languidly in the shade, where the thick turf,
Yet virgin from the kisses of the sun,
Retains some freshness, and I woo the wind

That still delays his coming. Why so slow,
Gentle and voluble spirit of the air?
Oh, come and breathe upon the fainting earth
Coolness and life. Is it that in his caves
He hears me? See, on yonder woody ridge,
The pine is bending his proud top, and now
Among the nearer groves, chestnut and oak
Are tossing their green boughs about. He comes;
Lo, where the grassy meadow runs in waves!
The deep distressful silence of the scene
Breaks up with mingling of unnumbered sounds
And universal motion. He is come,
Shaking a shower of blossoms from the shrubs,
And bearing on their fragrance; and he brings
Music of birds, and rustling of young boughs
And sound of swaying branches, and the voice
Of distant waterfalls. All the green herbs
Are stirring in his breath; a thousand flowers,
By the road-side and the borders of the brook,
Nod gayly to each other; glossy leaves
Are twinkling in the sun, as if the dew
Were on them yet, and silver waters break
Into small waves and sparkle as he comes.

WILLIAM CULLEN BRYANT (1794-1878)

Sonnet

Full many a glorious morning have I seen
Flatter the mountain-tops with sovereign eye,
Kissing with golden face the meadows green,
Gilding pale treams with heavenly alchemy.
Anon permit the basest clouds to ride
With ugly rack on his celestial face,
And from the forlorn world his visage hide,
Stealing unseen to west with this disgrace:
Even so my sun one early morn did shine
With all triumphant splendour on my brow;
But out! alack! he was but one hour mine,
The region cloud hath mask'd him from me now.
Yet him for this my love no whit disdaineth;
Suns of the world may stain, when heaven's sun staineth.

WILLIAM SHAKESPEARE (1564-1616)

from *The Testament of Beauty*

Or as I well remember one highday in June
bright on the seaward South-downs, where I had come afar
on a wild garden planted years agone, and fenced
thickly within live-beechen walls: the season it was
of prodigal gay blossom, and man's skill had made
a fair-order'd husbandry of that native pleasaunce:
But had there been no more than earth's wild loveliness,
the blue sky and the soft air and the unknown flowersprent lawns,
I would have lain me down and long'd, as then I did,
to lie there ever indolently undisturb'd, and watch
the common flowers that starr'd the fine grass of the wold,
waving in gay display their gold-heads to the sun,
each telling of its own inconscient happiness,
each type a faultless essence of God's will, such gems
as magic master-minds in painting or music
threw aside once for man's regard or disregard;
things supreme in themselves, eternal, unnumber'd
in the unexplored necessities of Life and Love.

ROBERT BRIDGES (1844-1930)

For Samuel Palmer

The countryside is wet and cold.
The lambs are gathered in the fold.
Tax-dodgers run the funny farms.
The nightingale exerts its charms.
Those labourers are very thick.
The setting sun illumes the rick.

Clods are dull clods and loam is loam.
Peace blesses ev'ry cottage home.
The rural rapes ride after dark.
Lightly ascends the twitt'ring lark.
Beer is expensive and not good.
Badgers play in the moonlit wood.

Mindless Nature doesn't care.
Through fields of stubble runs the hare.
Village idiots are grotesque.
The humble cot is picturesque.
Most farming is a frantic fiddle.
Rustic life's a timeless idyll.

GAVIN EWART (b 1916)

Conservation Piece

The countryside must be preserved!
(Preferably miles away from me.)
Neat hectares of the stuff reserved
For those in need of flower or tree.

I'll make do with landscape painting
Film documentaries on TV.
And when I need to escape, panting,
Then open-mouthed I'll head for the sea.

Let others stroll and take their leisure,
In grasses wade up to their knees,
For I derive no earthly pleasure
From the green green rash that makes me sneeze.

ROGER McGOUGH (b 1937)

After Sunset

The vast and solemn company of clouds
Around the Sun's death, lit, incarnadined,
Cool into ashy wan; as Night enshrouds
The level pasture, creeping up behind
Through voiceless vales, o'er lawn and purpled hill
And hazèd mead, her mystery to fulfil.
Cows low from far-off farms; the loitering wind
Sighs in the hedge, you hear it if you will, –
Though all the wood, alive atop with wings
Lifting and sinking through the leafy nooks,
Seethes with the clamour of ten thousand rooks.
Now every sound at length is hush'd away.
These few are sacred moments. One more Day
Drops in the shadowy gulf of bygone things.

WILLIAM ALLINGHAM (1824-1889)

A Summer Twilight

It is a Summer gloaming, balmy-sweet,
A gloaming brighten'd by an infant moon,
Fraught with the fairest light of middle June;
The lonely garden echoes to my feet,
And hark! O hear I not the gentle dews,
Fretting the silent forest in his sleep?
Or does the stir of housing insects creep
Thus faintly on mine ear? Day's many hues,
Waned with the paling light and are no more,
And none but drowsy pinions beat the air:
The bat is hunting softly by my door,
And, noiseless as the snow-flake, leaves his lair;
O'er the still copses flitting here and there,
Wheeling the self-same circuit o'er and o'er.

CHARLES TENNYSON TURNER (1808-1879)

Mild the Mist upon the Hill

Mild the mist upon the hill,
Telling not of storms to-morrow;
No; the day has wept its fill,
Spent its store of silent sorrow.

Oh, I'm gone back to the days of youth,
I am a child once more;
And 'neath my father's sheltering roof,
And near the old hall door,

I watch this cloudy evening fall,
After a day of rain:
Blue mists, sweet mists of summer pall
The horizon's mountain-chain.

The damp stands in the long, green grass
As thick as morning's tears;
And dreamy scents of fragrance pass
That breathe of other years.

EMILY BRONTË (1820-1849)

Halvergate marsh
rej84

A Summer's Morning

As one who long in populous city pent,
Where houses thick and sewers annoy the air,
Forth issuing on a summer's morn to breathe
Among the pleasant villages and farms
Adjoined, from each thing met conceives delight;
The smell of grain, or tedded grass, or kine,
Or dairy, each rural sight, each rural sound;
If chance, with nymphlike step, fair virgin pass,
What pleasing seemed, for her now pleases more;
She most, and in her look sums all delight.

JOHN MILTON (1608-1674)

The Passionate Shepherd to His Love

Come live with me and be my Love,
And we will all the pleasures prove
That valleys, groves, hills, and fields,
Woods, or steepy mountains yields.

And we will sit upon the rocks
Seeing the shepherds feed their flocks,
By shallow rivers, to whose falls
Melodious birds sing madrigals.

And I will make thee beds of roses
And a thousand fragrant posies,
A cap of flowers, and a kirtle
Embroidered all with leaves of myrtle;

A gown made of the finest wool,
Which from our pretty lambs we pull;
Fair lined slippers for the cold,
With buckels of the purest gold;

A belt of straw and ivy buds
With coral clasps and amber studs;
And if these pleasures may thee move,
Come live with me and be my Love.

The shepherd swains shall dance and sing
For thy delight each May morning:
If these delights thy mind may move,
Then live with me and be my Love.

CHRISTOPHER MARLOWE (1564-1593)

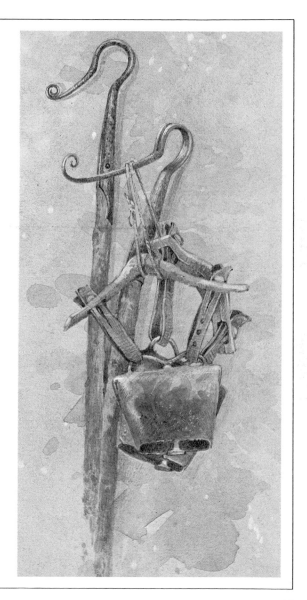

The Waggon-maker

I have made tales in verse, but this man made
Waggons of elm to last a hundred years;
The blacksmith forged the rims and iron gears,
His was the magic that the wood obeyed.

Each deft device that country wisdom bade,
Or farmers' practice needed, he preserved.
He wrought the subtle contours, straight and curved,
Only by eye, and instinct of the trade.

No weakness, no offence in any part,
It stood the strain in mired fields and roads
In all a century's struggle for its bread;
Bearing, perhaps, eight thousand heavy loads.
Beautiful always as a work of art,
Homing the bride, and harvest, and men dead.

JOHN MASEFIELD (1878-1967)

High Summer

I never wholly feel that summer is high,
However green the trees, or loud the birds,
However movelessly eye-winking herds
Stand in field ponds, or under large trees lie,
Till I do climb all cultured pastures by,
That hedged by hedgerows studiously fretted trim,
Smile like a lady's face with lace laced prim,
And on some moor or hill that seeks the sky
Lonely and nakedly, – utterly lie down,
And feel the sunshine throbbing on body and limb,
My drowsy brain in pleasant drunkenness swim,
Each rising thought sink back and dreamily drown,
Smiles creep o'er my face, and smother my lips, and cloy,
Each muscle sink to itself, and separately enjoy.

EBENEZER JONES (1820-1860)

On the Grasshopper and Cricket

The poetry of earth is never dead:
When all the birds are faint with the hot sun,
And hide in cooling trees, a voice will run
From hedge to hedge about the new-mown mead;
That is the Grasshopper's – he takes the lead
In summer luxury, – he has never done
With his delights; for when tired out with fun
He rests at ease beneath some pleasant weed.
The poetry of earth is ceasing never:
On a lone winter evening, when the frost
Has wrought a silence, from the stove there shrills
The Cricket's song, in warmth increasing ever,
And seems to one in drowsiness half lost,
The Grasshopper's among some grassy hills.

JOHN KEATS (1795-1821)

Day-Dreams

Broad August burns in milky skies,
The world is blanched with hazy heat;
The vast green pasture, even, lies
Too hot and bright for eyes and feet.

Amid the grassy levels rears
The sycamore against the sun
The dark boughs of a hundred years,
The emerald foliage of one.

Lulled in a dream of shade and sheen,
Within the clement twilight thrown
By that great cloud of floating green,
A horse is standing, still as stone.

He stirs nor head nor hoof, although
The grass is fresh beneath the branch;
His tail alone swings to and fro
In graceful curves from haunch to haunch.

He stands quite lost, indifferent
To rack or pasture, trace or rein;
He feels the vaguely sweet content
Of perfect sloth in limb and brain.

WILLIAM CANTON (1845-1926)

The Lofty Sky

To-day I want the sky,
The tops of the high hills,
Above the last man's house,
His hedges, and his cows,
Where, if I will, I look
Down even on sheep and rook,
And of all things that move
See buzzards only above: –
Past all trees, past furze
And thorn, where nought deters
The desire of the eye
For sky, nothing but sky.
I sicken of the woods
And all the multitudes
Of hedge-trees. They are no more
Than weeds upon this floor
Of the river of air

Leagues deep, leagues wide, where
I am like a fish that lives
In weeds and mud and gives
What's above him no thought.
I might be a tench for aught
That I can do to-day
Down on the wealden clay.
Even the tench has days
When he floats up and plays
Among the lily leaves
And sees the sky, or grieves
Not if he nothing sees:
While I, I know that trees
Under the lofty sky
Are weeds, fields mud, and I
Would arise and go far
To where the lilies are.

EDWARD THOMAS (1878-1917)

from *The Cloud*

I bring fresh showers for the thirsting flowers,
From the seas and the streams;
I bear light shade for the leaves when laid
In their noonday dreams.
From my wings are shaken the dews that waken
The sweet-buds every one,
When rocked to rest on their mother's breast,
As she dances about the sun.
I wield the flail of the lashing hail,
And whiten the green plains under,
And then again I dissolve it in rain,
And laugh as I pass in thunder . . .

I am the daughter of Earth and Water,
And the nursling of the Sky;
I pass through the pores of the ocean and shores;
I change, but I cannot die.
For after the rain when with never a stain
The pavilion of Heaven is bare,
And the winds and sunbeams with their convex gleams
Build up the blue dome of air,
I silently laugh at my own cenotaph,
And out of the caverns of rain,
Like a child from the womb, like a ghost from the tomb,
I arise and unbuild it again.

PERCY BYSSHE SHELLEY (1792-1822)

Cloud

Never alone
While over unending sky
Clouds move for ever.
Calling them beautiful
Humanity is in love with creatures of mist.
Born on the wind they rest,
Tenuous, without surface,
Passive stream from shape to shape,
Being with being melting breast with cloudy breast.
Ah could we like these
In freedom move in peace on the commotion of the air,
Never to return to what we are.
Made, unmade, remade, at rest in change,
From visible to invisible they pass
Or gather over the desolate hills
Veils of forgetfulness,
Or with reflected splendour evening gray
Charged with fiery gold and burning rose,
Their watery shapes shrines of the sun's glory.

KATHLEEN RAINE (1935-1980)

A Wish

Mine be a cot beside the hill;
A bee-hive's hum shall soothe my ear;
A willowy brook that turns a mill,
With many a fall shall linger near.

The swallow, oft, beneath my thatch
Shall twitter from her clay-built nest;
Oft shall the pilgrim lift the latch,
And share my meal, a welcome guest.

Around my ivied porch shall spring
Each fragrant flower that drinks the dew;
And Lucy, at her wheel, shall sing
In russet-gown and apron blue.

The village-church among the trees,
Where first our marriage-vows were given,
With merry peals shall swell the breeze
And point with taper spire to Heaven.

SAMUEL ROGERS (1763-1855)

The Hollow Wood

Out in the sun the goldfinch flits
Along the thistle-tops, flits and twits
Above the hollow wood
Where birds swim like fish –
Fish that laugh and shriek –
To and fro, far below
In the pale hollow wood.

Lichen, ivy, and moss
Keep evergreen the trees
That stand half-flayed and dying,
And the dead trees on their knees
In dog's-mercury and moss:
And the bright twit of the goldfinch drops
Down there as he flits on thistle-tops.

EDWARD THOMAS (1878-1917)

from *I Stood Tip-toe*

Sometimes goldfinches one by one will drop
From low hung branches; little space they stop;
But sip, and twitter, and their feathers sleek;
Then off at once, as in a wanton freak:
Or perhaps, to show their black and golden wings,
Pausing upon their yellow flutterings.

JOHN KEATS (1795-1821)

Of Birds and Birders

Better one bird in hand than ten in the wood:
Better for birders, but for birds not so good.

JOHN HEYWOOD (c.1497-c.1580)

The Housekeeper

The frugal snail, with forecast of repose,
Carries his house with him where'er he goes;
Peeps out, – and if there comes a shower of rain,
Retreats to his small domicile again.
Touch but a tip of him, a horn, – 'tis well, –
He curls up in his sanctuary shell.
He's his own landlord, his own tenant; stay
Long as he will, he dreads no Quarter Day.

Himself he boards and lodges; both invites
And feasts himself; sleeps with himself o' nights.
He spares the upholsterer trouble to procure
Chattels; himself is his own furniture,
And his sole riches. Whereso'er he roam, –
Knock when you will, – he's sure to be at home.

CHARLES LAMB (1775-1834)

Upon the Snail

She goes but softly, but she goeth sure;
She stumbles not as stronger creatures do:
Her journey's shorter, so she may endure
Better than they which do much further go.

She makes no noise, but stilly seizeth on
The flower or herb appointed for her food,
The which she quietly doth feed upon,
While others range, and gare, but find no good.

And though she doth but very softly go,
However 'tis not fast, nor slow, but sure;
And certainly they that do travel so,
The prize they do aim at they do procure.

JOHN BUNYAN (1628-1688)

The Snail

I praise the solemn snail
For when he walks abroad
He drags a slow and glistening trail
Behind him on the road.

Clock ticks for him in vain;
Tick tick tick – will he run?
He hankers not to share men's pain
Of losing to the sun.

Snail keeps a steady pace,
Therefore I honour snail;
For if none saw him win a race
None ever saw him fail.

You say, But in the end
He fills a thrush's throat.
A life, how could one better spend
Than for a song's top-note?

Flesh, sinew, blood and bone,
All that of me is strong,
Blithely would I bury in one
Short-lived immortal song.

ANDREW YOUNG (1885-1971)

Inscription for the Entrance to a Wood

Stranger, if thou hast learned a truth which needs
No school of long experience, that the world
Is full of guilt and misery and hast seen
Enough of all its sorrows, crimes, and cares,
To tire thee of it, enter this wild wood
And view the haunts of Nature. The calm shade
Shall bring a kindred calm, and the sweet breeze
That makes the green leaves dance, shall waft a balm
To thy sick heart. Thou wilt find nothing here
Of all that pained thee in the haunts of men,
And made thee loathe thy life. The primal curse
Fell, it is true, upon the unsinning earth,
But not in vengeance. God hath yoked to guilt
Her pale tormentor, misery. Hence, these shades
Are still the abodes of gladness; the thick roof
Of green and stirring branches is alive
And musical with birds that sing and sport
In wantonness of spirit; while below
The squirrel, with raised paws and form erect,
Chirps merrily. Throngs of insects in the shade
Try their thin wings and dance in the warm beam

That waked them into life. Even the green trees
Partake the deep contentment; as they bend
To the soft winds, the sun from the blue sky
Looks in and sheds a blessing on the scene.
Scarce less the cleft-born wild-flower seems to enjoy
Existence than the wingèd plunderer
That sucks its sweets. The mossy rocks themselves,
And the old and ponderous trunks of prostrate trees
That lead from knoll to knoll a causey rude
Or bridge the sunken brook, and their dark roots,
With all their earth upon them, twisting high,
Breathe fixed tranquillity. The rivulet
Sends forth glad sounds, and tripping o'er its bed
Of pebbly sands, or leaping down the rocks,
Seems, with continuous laughter, to rejoice
In its own being. Softly tread the marge,
Lest from her midway perch thou scare the wren
That dips her bill in water. The cool wind,
That stirs the stream in play, shall come to thee,
Like one that loves thee nor will let thee pass
Ungreeted, and shall give its light embrace.

WILLIAM CULLEN BRYANT (1794-1878)

Fox

Who
Wears the smartest evening dress in England?
Checks his watch by the stars
And hurries, white-scarfed,
To the opera
In the flea-ridden hen-house
Where he will conduct the orchestra?

Who
With a Robin Hood mask over his eyes
Meets King Pheasant the Magnificent
And with silent laughter
Shakes all the gold out of his robes
Then carries him bodily home
Over his shoulder,
A swag-bag?

And who
Flinging back his Dracula cloak
And letting one fang wink in the moonlight
Lifts off his top hat
Shows us the moon through the bottom of it
Then brings out of it, in a flourish of feathers,
The gander we locked up at sunset?

TED HUGHES (b 1930)

Hurrahing in Harvest

Summer ends now; now, barbarous in beauty, the stooks rise
Around; up above, what wind-walks! what lovely behaviour
Of silk-sack clouds! has wilder, wilful-wavier
Meal-drift moulded ever and melted across skies?

I wálk, I líft up, I lift úp heart, éyes,
Down all that glory in the heavens to glean our Saviour;
And, éyes, heárt, what looks, what lips yet gáve you a
Rapturous love's greeting of realer, of rounder replies?

And the azurous hung hills are his world-wielding shoulder
Majestic – as a stallion stalward, very-violet-sweet! –
These things, these things were here and but the beholder
Wánting: which two whén they ónce méet,
The heart réars wíngs bold and bolder
And hurls for him, O half hurls earth for him off under his feet.

GERARD MANLEY HOPKINS (1844-1889)

Sunset and Sunrise

Another and another and another
And still another sunset and sunrise,
The same yet different, different yet the same,
Seen by me now in my declining years
As in my early childhood, youth and manhood;
And by my parents and my parents' parents,
And by the parents of my parents' parents,
And by their parents counted back for ever,
Seen, all their lives long, even as now by me;
And by my children and my children's children
And by the children of my children's children
And by their children counted on for ever
Still to be seen as even now seen by me;
Clear and bright sometimes, sometimes dark and clouded
But still the same sunsetting and sunrise;
The same for ever to the never ending
Line of observers, to the same observer
Through all the changes of his life the same:
Sunsetting and sunrising and sunsetting,
And then again sunrising and sunsetting,
Sunrising and sunsetting evermore.

JAMES HENRY (1798-1876)

Progress of Evening

From yonder wood, mark blue-eyed Eve proceed:
First through the deep and warm and secret glens,
Through the pale glimmering privet-scented lane,
And through those alders by the river-side:
Now the soft dust impedes her, which the sheep
Have hollow'd out beneath their hawthorn shade.
But ah! look yonder! see a misty tide
Rise up the hill, lay low the frowning grove,
Enwrap the gay white mansion, sap its sides
Until they sink and melt away like chalk;
Now it comes down against our village-tower,
Covers its base, floats o'er its arches, tears
The clinging ivy from the battlements,
Mingles in broad embrace the obdurate stone,
(All one vast ocean) and goes swelling on
In slow and silent, dim and deepening waves.

W.S. LANDOR (1775-1864)

Twilight

Darkness comes out of the earth
And swallows dip into the pallor of the west;
From the hay comes the clamour of children's mirth;
Wanes the old palimpsest.

The night-stock oozes scent,
And a moon-blue moth goes flittering by:
All that the worldly day has meant
Wastes like a lie.

D.H. LAWRENCE (1885-1930)

Sunset Wings

To-night this sunset spreads two golden wings
Cleaving the western sky;
Wing'd too with wind it is, and winnowings
Of birds; as if the day's last hour in rings
Of strenuous flight must die.

Sun-steeped in fire, the homeward pinions sway
Above the dovecote-tops;
And clouds of starlings, ere they rest with day,
Sink, clamorous like mill-waters, at wild play,
By turns in every copse:

Each tree heart-deep the wrangling rout receives, –
Save for the whirr within,
You could not tell the starlings from the leaves;
Then one great puff of wings, and the swarm heaves
Away with all its din.

DANTE GABRIEL ROSSETTI (1828-1882)

The Fall of Day

Torn wings of flame are wafting down the sky
Pinioned like sweeping scythes now idly hanging at rest;
The soft clustered shoulder-feathers in rosy confusion lie
Helpless; another day has flown too high
And falls wingless, blood streaming through its yellow hair,
    headlong into the west.

Slowly the wings of Day are eddying lower
Their feathers lifeless, and the rose lights turning to gray.
No longer they sweep the hours, as the scythe of the mower
Hisses through the flowers; the timid night-airs blow
A cool ointment over the earth, blistered in the flight of Day.

Our overweening Days strive too far, till the heat and the sweat
Sicken us, and we are stunned by the rushings of the labouring wings.
And then all our days in a plunge of death pay the debt
Of their vain up-striving, and night remains for regret
And the ignoble prayers of the panic-stricken whom darkness enrings.

D.H. LAWRENCE (1885-1930)

The Jackdaw

There is a bird who, by his coat,
And by the hoarseness of his note,
Might be suppos'd a crow;
A great frequenter of the church,
Where, bishop-like, he finds a perch,
And dormitory too.

Above the steeple shines a plate,
That turns and turns, to indicate
From what point blows the weather.
Look up – your brains begin to swim,
'Tis in the clouds – that pleases him,
He chooses it the rather.

Fond of the speculative height,
Thither he wings his airy flight,
And thence securely sees
The bustle and the raree-show
That occupy mankind below,
Secure and at his ease.

You think, no doubt, he sits and muses
On future broken bones and bruises,
If he should chance to fall.
No; not a single thought like that
Employs his philosophic pate,
Or troubles it at all.

He sees, that this great roundabout –
The world, with all its motley rout,
Church, army, physic, law,
Its customs, and its bus'nesses, –
Is no concern at all of his,
And says – what says he? – Caw.

Thrice happy bird! I too have seen
Much of the vanities of men;
And, sick of having seen 'em,
Would cheerfully these limbs resign
For such a pair of wings as thine,
And such a head between 'em.

WILLIAM COWPER (1731-1800)

Nutting

It seems a day,
(I speak of one from many singled out)
One of those heavenly days which cannot die,
When forth I sallied from our cottage-door,
And with a wallet o'er my shoulder slung,
A nutting crook in hand, I turn'd my steps
Towards the distant woods, a Figure quaint,
Trick'd out in proud disguise of Beggar's woods
Put on for the occasion, by advice
And exhortation of my frugal Dame.
Motley accoutrement! of power to smile
At thorns, and brakes, and brambles, and, in truth,
More ragged than need was. Among the woods,
And o'er the pathless rocks, I forc'd my way
Until, at length, I came to one dear nook
Unvisited, where not a broken bough
Droop'd with its wither'd leaves, ungracious sign
Of devastation, but the hazels rose
Tall and erect, with milk-white clusters hung,
A virgin scene! – A little while I stood,
Breathing with such suppression of the heart
As joy delights in; and with wise restraint
Voluptuous, fearless of a rival, eyed
The banquet, or beneath the trees I sate
Among the flowers, and with the flowers I play'd;
A temper known to those, who, after long
And weary expectation, have been bless'd
With sudden happiness beyond all hope. –

– Perhaps it was a bower beneath whose leaves
The violets of five seasons re-appear
And fade, unseen by any human eye,
Where fairy water-breaks do murmur on
For ever, and I saw the sparkling foam,
And with my cheek on one of those green stones
That, fleec'd with moss, beneath the shady trees,
Lay round me scatter'd like a flock of sheep,
I heard the murmur and the murmuring sound,
In that sweet mood when pleasure loves to pay
Tribute to ease, and, of its joy secure
The heart luxuriates with indifferent things,
Wasting its kindliness on stocks and stones,
And on the vacant air. Then up I rose,
And dragg'd to earth both branch and bough, with crash
And merciless ravage; and the shady nook
Of hazels, and the green and mossy bower
Deform'd and sullied, patiently gave up
Their quiet being: and unless I now
Confound my present feelings with the past,
Even then, when from the bower I turn'd away,
Exulting, rich beyond the wealth of kings
I felt a sense of pain when I beheld
The silent trees and the intruding sky. –

Then, dearest Maiden! move along these shades
In gentleness of heart with gentle hand
Touch, – for there is a Spirit in the woods.

WILLIAM WORDSWORTH (1770-1850)

After Rain

The rain of a night and a day and a night
Stops at the light
Of this pale choked day. The peering sun
Sees what has been done.
The road under the trees has a border new
Of purple hue
Inside the border of bright thin grass:
For all that has
Been left by November of leaves is torn
From hazel and thorn
And the greater trees. Throughout the copse
No dead leaf drops
On grey grass, green moss, burnt-orange fern,
At the wind's return:
The leaflets out of the ash-tree shed
Are thinly spread
In the road, like little black fish, inlaid,
As if they played.
What hangs from the myriad branches down there
So hard and bare
Is twelve yellow apples lovely to see
On one crab-tree.
And on each twig of every tree in the dell
Uncountable
Crystals both dark and bright of the rain
That begins again.

EDWARD THOMAS (1878-1917)

Autumn Idleness

This sunlight shames November where he grieves
In dead red leaves, and will not let him shun
The day, though bough with bough be over-run.
But with a blessing every glade receives
High salutation; while from hillock-eaves
The deer gaze calling, dappled white and dun,
As if, being foresters of old, the sun
Had marked them with the shade of forest-leaves.

Here dawn to-day unveiled her magic glass;
Here noon now gives the thirst and takes the dew;
Till eve bring rest when other good things pass.
And here the lost hours the lost hours renew
While I still lead my shadow o'er grass,
Nor know, for longing, that which I should do.

DANTE GABRIEL ROSSETTI (1828-1882)

The Owl

Downhill I came, hungry, and yet not starved;
Cold, yet had heat within me that was proof
Against the North wind; tired, yet so that rest
Had seemed the sweetest thing under a roof
Then at the inn I had food, fire, and rest,
Knowing how hungry, cold, and tired was I.
All of the night was quite barred out except
An owl's cry, a most melancholy cry

Shaken out long and clear upon the hill,
No merry note, nor cause of merriment,
But one telling me plain what I escaped
And others could not, that night, as in I went.
And salted was my food, and my repose,
Salted and sobered, too, by the bird's voice
Speaking for all who lay under the stars,
Soldiers and poor, unable to rejoice.

EDWARD THOMAS (1878-1917)

from *The Task*

No noise is here, or none that hinders thought.
The redbreast warbles still, but is content
With slender notes, and more than half suppressed:
Pleased with his solitude, and flitting light
From spray to spray, where'er he rests he shakes
From many a twig the pendant drops of ice,
That tinkle in the withered leaves below.

WILLIAM COWPER (1731-1800)

from *Winter*

. . . The fowls of heaven,
Tamed by the cruel season, crowd around
The winnowing store, and claim the little boon
Which Providence assigns them. One alone,
The redbreast, sacred to the household gods,
Wisely regardful of the embroiling sky,
In joyless fields and thorny thickets leaves
His shivering mates, and pays to trusted man
His annual visit. Half afraid, he first
Against the window beats; then brisk alights
On the warm hearth; then, hopping o'er the floor,
Eyes all the smiling family askance,
And pecks, and starts, and wonders where he is —
Till, more familiar grown, the table crumbs
Attract his slender feet . . .

JAMES THOMSON (1700-1748)

Winter Nightfall

The day begins to droop, —
Its course is done:
But nothing tells the place
Of the setting sun.

The hazy darkness deepens,
And up the lane
You may hear, but cannot see,
The homing wain.

An engine pants and hums
In the farm hard by:
Its lowering smoke is lost
In the lowering sky.

The soaking branches drip,
And all night through
The dropping will not cease
In the avenue.

A tall man there in the house
Must keep his chair:
He knows he will never again
Breathe the spring air:

His heart is worn with work;
He is giddy and sick
If he rise to go as far
As the nearest rick:

He thinks of his morn of life,
His hale, strong years;
And braves as he may the night
Of darkness and tears.

ROBERT BRIDGES (1844-1930)

Snowflakes

Out of the bosom of the Air,
Out of the cloud-folds of her garments shaken,
Over the woodlands brown and bare,
Over the harvest-fields forsaken,
Silent, and soft, and slow
Descends the snow.

Even as our cloudy fancies take
Suddenly shape in some divine expression,
Even as the troubled heart doth make
In the white countenance confession,
The troubled sky reveals
The grief it feels.

This is the poem of the Air,
Slowly in silent syllables recorded;
This is the secret of despair,
Long in its cloudy bosom hoarded,
Now whispered and revealed
To wood and field.

HENRY WADSWORTH LONGFELLOW (1807-1882)

Sheep in Winter

The sheep get up and make their many tracks
And bear a load of snow upon their backs,
And gnaw the frozen turnip to the ground
With sharp quick bite, and then go noising round
The boy that pecks the turnips all the day
And knocks his hands to keep the cold away
And laps his legs in straw to keep them warm
And hides behind the hedges from the storm.
The sheep, as tame as dogs, go where he goes
And try to shake their fleeces from the snows,
Then leave their frozen meal and wander round
The stubble stack that stands beside the ground,
And lie all night and face the drizzling storm
And shun the hovel where they might be warm.

JOHN CLARE (1793-1864)

A Frosty Day

Grass afield wears silver thatch;
Palings all are edged with rime;
Frost-flowers pattern round the latch;
Cloud nor breeze dissolve the clime:

When the waves are solid floor,
And the clods are iron-bound,
And the boughs are crystall'd hoar,
And the red leaf nailed aground.

When the fieldfare's flight is slow,
And a rosy vapour rim,
Now the sun is small and low,
Belts along the region dim.

When the ice-crack flies and flaws,
Shore to shore, with thunder shock,
Deeper then the evening daws,
Clearer than the village clock.

When the rusty blackbird strips,
Bunch by bunch, the coral thorn;
And the pale day-crescent dips,
New to heaven, a slender horn.

JOHN LEICESTER WARREN, LORD DE TABLEY (1835-1895)

Tintern Abbey

I have learned
To look on nature, not as in the hour
Of thoughtless youth, but hearing oftentimes
The still, sad music of humanity,
Not harsh nor grating, though of ample power
To chasten and subdue. And I have felt
A presence that disturbs me with the joy
Of elevated thoughts; a sense sublime
Of something far more deeply interfused,
Whose dwelling is the light of setting suns,
And the round ocean and the living air,
And the blue sky, and in the mind of man:
A motion and a spirit, that impels
All thinking things, all objects of all thought,
And rolls through all things. Therefore am I still
A lover of the meadows and the woods,
And mountains; and of all that we behold
From this green earth; of all the mighty world
Of eye, and ear, – both what they half create,
And what perceive; well pleased to recognize
In nature and the language of the sense
The anchor of my purest thoughts.

WILLIAM WORDSWORTH (1770-1850)